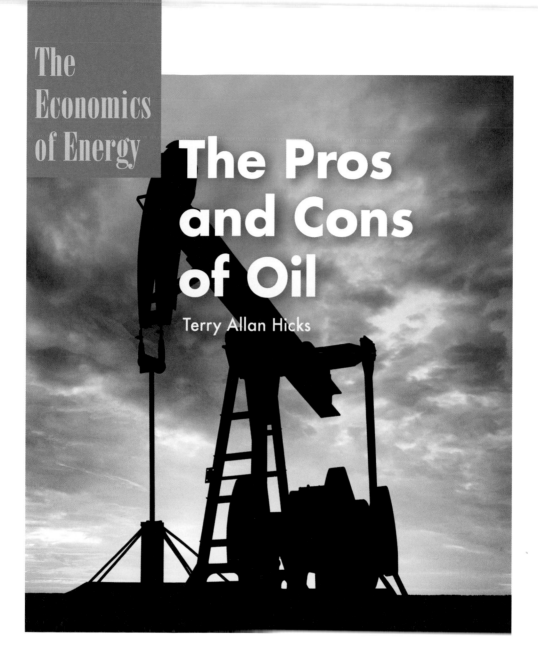

The Economics of Energy

The Pros and Cons of Oil

Terry Allan Hicks

Cavendish Square

New York

For my son John, whose passion for the environment and alternative energy has helped to shape my thinking on many of the issues discussed in this book.

Published in 2015 by Cavendish Square Publishing, LLC
243 5th Avenue, Suite 136, New York, NY 10016

Library of Congress Cataloging-in-Publication Data

Hicks, Terry Allan.
The pros and cons of oil / Terry Allan Hicks.
    pages cm. — (The economics of energy)
Includes index.
ISBN 978-1-62712-927-5 (hardcover) ISBN 978-1-62712-929-9 (ebook)
1. Petroleum industry and trade—Juvenile literature. 2. Petroleum—Juvenile literature. 3. Energy consumption—Juvenile literature. I. Title.

HD9565.H486 2015
338.2'7282—dc23

2013050654

Editorial Director: Dean Miller
Editor: Kristen Susienka
Copy Editor: Cynthia Roby
Art Director: Jeffrey Talbot
Designer: Amy Greenan
Production Manager: Jennifer Ryder-Talbot
Production Editor: David McNamara
Photo Researcher: J8 Media

The photographs in this book are used by permission and through the courtesy of: Cover by Amarate Tansawet Gift of Light/Flickr/Getty Images; Ralf Hettler/E+/Getty Images, 1; Ken Biggs/The Image Bank/Getty Images, 4; Konrad Summers from Santa Clarita (Valencia), California, USA/File:Wooden Derick–Kern West Oil Museum (3355730344).jpg/Wikimedia Commons, 6, 8, 25, 28, 41, 48, 52, 59, 73; Keren Su/China Span/Getty Images, 9; Unknown/File:Hartmann Maschinenhalle 1868 (01).jpg/Wikimedia Commons, 10–11; Unknownроды они виноваты во всём/File:Deepwater Horizon offshore drilling unit on fire 2010.jpg/Wikimedia Commons, 12; Walter Siegmund/File:Anacortes Refinery 31911.jpg/Wikimedia Commons, 13; Hulton Archive/Getty Images, 14; Hulton Archive/Archive Photos/Getty Images, 15; Thomas Hartwell/Time & Life Pictures/Getty Images, 18–19; Warren K. Leffler/File:Line at a gas station, June 15, 1979.jpg/Wikimedia Commons, 21; ©AP Photo/ Sergei Grits/FILE, 22; The Asahi Shimbun/Getty Images, 24–25; John Morgan from Walnut Creek, CA, USA/File:BIG Wheel (3327257572).jpg/Wikimedia Commons, 26; Bloomberg/Getty Images, 29; Joshua Doubek/File:Drilling the Bakken formation in the Williston Basin.jpg/Wikimedia Commons, 29; AP Photo/U.S. Coast Guard, 30; J. Patrick Fischer/File:2012 Pudong.jpg/Wikimedia Commons, 34–35; US Department of the Interior Image Library, 35; Steve Wilson from Orpington, UK/File:Shepherds Flat Wind Farm 2011.jpg/Wikimedia Commons, 36; Fotokostic/Shutterstock. com, 37; Bloomberg/Getty Images, 38–39; idreamstock/age fotostock, 42; Wofratz/File:Nuclearice-breakeryamal.jpg/Wikimedia Commons, 44; Jochem Wijnands/Horizons WWP/age fotostock, 46–47; US Air Force/File:USAF F-16A F-15C F-15E Desert Storm edit2.jpg/Wikimedia Commons, 50–51; Emily Beament/AP Images, 53; M 93/File:Toyota Prius Life (ZVW30) front-2 20110116.jpg/Wikimedia Commons, 55; A. Bakker/File:PaleisstraatAmsterdam.jpg/Wikimedia Commons, 56; Craig Cozart/E+/ Getty Images, 60; Maximilian Stock Ltd./Oxford Scientific/Getty Images, 60; Henry Georgi/All Canada Photos/Getty Images, 60–61; tentan/iStock/Thinkstock, 62; UNclimatechange from Bonn, Germany/File:COP18 Doha 2012.jpg/Wikimedia Commons, 66–67; Bloomberg/Getty Images, 69; Jupiterimages/Pixland/Thinkstock, 71.

Printed in the United States of America

The Economics of Energy

Table of Contents

Oil has a huge impact—economic and environmental—on the world we live in.

Chapter 1

The History of Oil

O il is everywhere in our daily lives. It powers the cars we drive as well as the trucks, trains, ships, and aircraft that carry the goods we purchase. It fuels many of the power plants that supply our homes, office buildings, and factories with light and heat. Oil is also an important ingredient in many everyday household products. Our ever-increasing need for oil, and for a steady, secure supply of it, has a powerful impact on world events. Wars have been fought for oil, and won or lost because one side had more or less of it. And yet, for most of human history, this now-precious resource lay beneath the Earth's surface, almost unnoticed by the millions living above it.

How Oil Is Created

Oil results from the remains of prehistoric plants and animals, including microscopic organisms such as algae and plankton, that died and decayed on ancient seabeds as much as 600 million years ago. Many of those seas have long disappeared, becoming dry land. The organic material left behind by these long-dead organisms, which had absorbed and stored

A DEEPER DIVE

Other Types of Oils

Many types of oils other than petroleum products have been, and continue to be, used all over the world. Oils made from fruits and vegetables, such as olive oil and peanut oil, are, in many regions, essential ingredients in cooking. Animal fats have been turned into oils and burned for light and heat and used to lubricate machines since prehistoric times. Lamps that burned oil from hunted animals have been found in caves in Europe and elsewhere dating back as far as 18,000 BCE. These lamps allowed early peoples to see well enough to make the beautiful cave paintings that have taught us much of what we know about their lives.

energy from the sun, was compressed and heated beneath several layers of rock. This process transformed the material into hydrocarbons, which are chemical compounds, in liquid, solid, or gas forms, made up of hydrogen and carbon atoms.

When hydrocarbons occur in liquid form, they are known as petroleum. There are two main types of petroleum: oil, a thick, heavy liquid; and **natural gas**, a mixture of hydrocarbon gases, usually found close to oil deposits. Other hydrocarbons include coal, a solid that can be burned in its raw form, and bitumen, a thick, tarlike substance now used mostly in road construction.

Oil, natural gas, and other hydrocarbons are often called fossil fuels, but this is technically incorrect, because they were formed from organisms that never became fossilized. Another common mistake is to refer to these organic substances as **minerals**.

When hydrocarbons are burned, they release their stored energy as light and heat. Oil and related fuels, such as natural gas, are some of the most powerful and efficient of all energy sources, but they are not **renewable resources**. Once they are burned, they are gone forever. Burning them also releases waste gases into the environment. This causes two serious problems that currently affect the entire world: the need for new fuel sources, and pollution, especially of the air, that results when the fuels are burned.

Oil Through the Ages

Oil was used in the ancient world, though usually not as an energy source. The Babylonians, who lived in present-day Iraq, now one of the

A DEEPER DIVE

Coal

The earliest hydrocarbon to be widely used as an energy source was coal. It was burned in prehistoric times for cooking and heating, but became truly important during the Industrial Revolution, which began in Europe in the late eighteenth century. The factories that were built during this period, and many of the products they manufactured, such as steam locomotives and steamships, were mostly powered by coal. But coal has a drawback that made it unsuitable for an increasingly industrialized modern economy: it is comparatively low in **energy content**. Because of this, coal-powered machinery requires extremely large amounts of the fuel, which is heavy and expensive to transport. A specific amount of gasoline, a fuel made from oil, produces almost twice as many **calories** as the same amount of coal.

The ancient Chinese used drilling techniques like the ones shown in this drawing to extract oil from the ground using bamboo tubes.

world's most important producers of oil, used it to waterproof their houses and boats. The Persians, from what is now Iran, another important oil-producing nation, used oil as a weapon. In 481 BCE, their armies attacked the Greek city of Athens with flaming arrows soaked in oil. By the fourth century BCE, the Chinese were drilling shallow oil wells and using hollow bamboo poles to bring the oil to the surface. In the Middle Ages, the Italian traveler Marco Polo witnessed people in Baku (in present-day Azerbaijan, in Central Asia) gathering oil from naturally formed seeps,

Early factories, like this one in Germany, needed more and more energy.

which are places where oil naturally permeates the Earth's surface, in one of the world's oldest and simplest methods of oil extraction.

In the 1800s, as factories and machines became more advanced, manufacturers, inventors, and engineers began to seek more, and more efficient, sources of energy. The most promising was oil. In the early nineteenth century, oil began to be widely used for outdoor lighting. Within a few years, gaslight, light made by burning illuminating gas, was considered a must on the streets of many modern cities. In homes, however, whale oil was more likely to be used for lighting, and a great number of whales were hunted for their oil. As the whale populations became smaller, whale oil became very expensive. But in the 1840s it began to be replaced by kerosene, an inexpensive lamp fuel **distilled** from oil, and whaling declined. The creation of kerosene may actually have saved some species of whales from extinction.

By the end of the nineteenth century, electricity was replacing kerosene as fuel for streetlights worldwide. (Today kerosene is mostly used as a base in aviation fuels.) But by then, the demand for oil was so great that the modern oil industry had already begun to take shape.

The Beginnings of the Oil Industry

The history of the oil business began in 1859 in Titusville, Pennsylvania, a town located alongside a stream now called Oil Creek. Edwin Drake, a retired railway conductor, drilled 70 feet (21 meters) beneath the surface and found what is thought to have been the first oil well in the United States. He managed to produce a steady supply of about 400 gallons of oil every 24 hours. Drake's discovery set off an intense surge of oil exploration that historians have compared to the great California gold rush (1848–1855). It also established the United States as the leader in worldwide oil exploration, an advantage the country continued to hold for many years.

Early oil exploration and extraction was difficult and dangerous. Oil wells often caught fire or exploded, injuring or killing the drilling crews. The environment was also damaged. When excess oil and oil **by-products** were dumped into nearby rivers and lakes, local water sources became contaminated. Conflicts, often violent or even deadly, erupted over the rights not only to drill at the most promising sites, but also to transport the

The disastrous fire on the offshore oil rig *Deepwater Horizon* in the Gulf of Mexico in 2010.

oil to where it was needed. Despite these problems, the potential financial gains kept the oil rush going.

Early oil producers faced a serious problem that remains today: the need to transport unrefined oil, referred to as crude oil, to **refineries**.

Crude oil has little value as an energy source until it is converted into fuel at refineries like this one.

There it could be turned into usable products and then delivered to its buyers. In the earliest days of the Pennsylvania oil fields, oil was stored in wooden whiskey barrels and transported via horse-drawn wagons—an extremely expensive and unreliable method. The need for improved transportation methods led to the creation of the first oil pipeline in the early 1860s. By the 1880s, pipelines connected the Pennsylvania oil fields with many eastern cities, including ports such as New York City. Tankers, ships built especially to carry large amounts of oil, were already carrying their cargoes far greater distances.

In the early days, many buyers did not trust the measured accuracy of the oil they were purchasing. To solve this problem, the oil barrel,

Spindletop, the gusher that set off the rush for "black gold" in Texas.

specifically designed to hold 42 U.S. gallons (159 liters), was created. The barrel remains the standard international measurement for oil today. It is difficult to estimate the exact amount of oil produced in the industry's early years, but by the early 1870s, worldwide production was probably about 6 million barrels per year. In 2012, the most recent year for which reliable statistics are available, production was 76 million barrels, an increase of approximately 1,167 percent.

Oil was beginning to be discovered and extracted in unexpected places—and in spectacular amounts. In 1896, the first offshore (underwater) oil well was drilled close to a dock in Summerland, California. In 1901, a huge amount of oil exploded from a drilling site near Beaumont, Texas. The gusher, named Spindletop for the hill where the site was located, created a forceful flow of oil reaching heights greater than 150 feet (46 m) and producing an astonishing 100,000 barrels of oil daily. In the years that followed, Texas and its neighboring states of Oklahoma and Louisiana became the country's most important sources of oil.

By the end of the nineteenth century, oil had already become an extremely valuable commodity, and oil exploration, extraction, and refining were extremely important industries. The first oil produced in the Pennsylvania fields sold for $18 per barrel, which equals about $450 in today's money. Today's prices vary depending on the oil's type and quality, but the current average is about $100 per barrel.

Ford workers put the finishing touches on a Model T in 1914.

The turning point for the oil industry came early in the beginning of the twentieth century, with the widespread use of the internal combustion engine. This highly efficient type of engine, which worked by causing liquid fuel to explode inside a closed chamber, had many uses. But none was more important than the automobile. The first automobiles were built in the 1880s, and early models were powered by everything from electricity to firewood to steam. The earliest automobiles were also extremely expensive. But in 1908, industrialist Henry Ford began mass production of his now-famous Model T, the first car that was affordable for many buyers.

Fuel from oil, because it is comparatively lightweight, also made possible the development of the airplane, which the Wright brothers had first flown successfully at Kitty Hawk, North Carolina, in 1903. Oil was also becoming the fuel of choice for long-range ships; oil-powered vessels rapidly replaced the coal-fired steamships that had dominated the world's oceans for more than half a century. This set the pattern for the single most important use of oil, which has remained constant to this day: the transportation of people and goods, by land, sea, and air.

The Worldwide Search for Oil

By the early twentieth century, oil and the products made from it were beginning to be recognized as strategically important. Inevitably, the nations of the world recognized that motorized vehicles could be used as weapons of war. Motorized tanks and aircraft were first widely used in battle during the First World War (1914–1918). As the conflict neared its end, oil shortages became a severe problem for both sides.

These shortages became a decisive factor in bringing the war to its close.

Even in the earliest days of the industry, many people were concerned that oil production, and the wealth and power resulting from it, were concentrated in too few hands. By the 1880s, one company, Standard Oil, was responsible for approximately 90 percent of the oil production in the United States. Its founder, John D. Rockefeller, was the richest person in the world. In 1911, the U.S. government ordered the dissolution, or breakup, of Standard Oil into thirty-three smaller companies. Those smaller companies, including BP, ExxonMobil, and Texaco, remain among the world's largest and most profitable businesses.

The overwhelming demand for energy sent oil explorers to more and more distant places, especially the Middle East, the region where oil had had its earliest uses. In 1938, American engineers working for Standard Oil discovered oil in Saudi Arabia. Today, Saudi Arabia produces about 11 percent of the world's oil. Many of its neighbors, including Iraq, Iran, and the other Persian Gulf countries, are also among the world's largest oil producers.

The worldwide demand for energy was also one of the primary causes of the Second World War (1939–1945). The Axis powers—which included Germany, Japan, and Italy—desperately needed oil to fuel their factories and military forces. This led Germany to invade oil-producing areas such as Romania and parts of North Africa, and the Japanese to conquer oil-rich regions including the Dutch colony that is now Indonesia. The inability to obtain sufficient fuel for their factories, aircraft, and other machinery of war was a major factor in the defeat of the Axis powers.

Oil's importance had begun to extend beyond energy. In 1935, Wallace Carothers, a research chemist with the chemical manufacturer DuPont,

A warship escorts an oil tanker through the Persian Gulf.

used hydrocarbons from oil to create the fiber known as nylon, the world's first commercially successful **synthetic** fabric. In 1951, researchers developed the first practical plastics—lightweight, flexible oil-based materials that are now used in items from soda bottles to spacecraft.

During the postwar period, oil production was becoming a worldwide industry. By this time, massive deposits of oil had been found in many parts of the world, including Russia (then part of the Soviet Union), Mexico, and Venezuela. The production of oil was especially important in the Middle East. However, U.S. and European companies dominated every aspect of the industry in the region, and also had great influence on the area's political developments. The Western powers believed that they needed a secure, stable source of oil. For this reason, they sometimes helped to overthrow democratically elected governments that threatened their control of the oil trade and replaced them with unpopular, oppressive rulers. This tactic, which was used in both Iran and Iraq in 1953 alone, created problems that still exist today, including great resentment against the United States.

The Politics of Oil

The oil-producing nations believed they needed a stronger voice in the control of the industry. In 1961, Iraq, Iran, Kuwait, Saudi Arabia, and Venezuela founded the Organization of Petroleum Exporting Countries (OPEC), a **cartel** designed to give them greater power in negotiating with oil buyers. In the coming years, OPEC was to exercise great power on the world stage. In October 1973, during a war between Israel and many of its Arab neighbors, some OPEC members stopped shipping oil to countries that were seen as supporting Israel.

This caused severe oil shortages in many parts of the world, including the United States. The price of oil products then increased enormously. This was because of the "law" of supply and demand, one of the basic principles of economics. If the supply of any product or service exceeds the demand for it, its price will fall. If demand exceeds supply, the price will rise. In a very short time, the cost of a barrel of oil in the United States increased 300 percent, to approximately $75 per barrel, and the price of gasoline increased to an unheard-of fifty-five cents per gallon. This "oil shock" caused a recession that brought on high unemployment lasting for a long time. A second oil crisis followed the 1979 revolution that overthrew Mohammad Reza Pahlavi, the Shah (Emperor) of Iran, who had been a close ally of the United States. This crisis caused similar shortages and huge price increases, and brought about another recession.

The world was more determined than ever to find more sources of oil. Industry observers were concerned about the concept of **peak oil**, meaning the point at which the demand for recoverable oil exceeds supply. Improved offshore exploration and drilling techniques made it possible to drill for oil in deeper waters, including the North Sea, the section of the Atlantic Ocean between Britain and Norway. The search for oil expanded to increasingly remote locations. In 1966, oil was discovered in Prudhoe Bay, on the North Slope of Alaska. By the mid 1980s, the North Slope was supplying about a quarter of the United States' oil production.

Oil and the Environment

The environmental impact of oil exploration, extraction, and transportation had become a subject of deep concern worldwide. In 1969, a blowout at an offshore oil rig near Santa Barbara, California, spewed almost 4 million gallons (15 million L) of crude oil into the Pacific Ocean. This resulted in severe damage to the nearby beaches and threatened the region's marine

During the 1979 oil crisis, cars and trucks lined up for hours for scarce gasoline supplies.

life. In 1989, the supertanker *Exxon Valdez* ran aground in Alaska's Prince William Sound, spilling 39,000 gallons of oil (150,000 L) across many miles of Arctic coastline. And in 2010, the *Deepwater Horizon*, a drilling rig in the Gulf of Mexico, caught fire and exploded, killing eleven workers and creating an underwater gusher that spewed an estimated 210 million gallons (800 million L) of crude oil in the water, devastating one of the world's most delicate **ecosystems**. These tragedies made it clear to the world that the true cost of oil far outweighed the price consumers paid for gasoline.

An even more serious concern was the air pollution caused by the burning of ever-increasing amounts of oil. Nineteenth-century cities were often shrouded in heavy clouds of coal smoke. But the widespread use of gasoline and other oil products made this problem far worse. By the 1960s, the quality of the air in most of the world's major cities was very poor. However, this situation began to improve, in part because of the oil price increases of the 1970s. People and businesses in many parts of the world began to reduce their oil consumption. They drove smaller, more fuel-efficient

A seabird coated with oil from a tanker accident.

automobiles and used alternative fuels. In many parts of the world, oil and hydrocarbon products were taxed, which greatly decreased consumption in those markets. By the 1990s, air and water in many parts of the world had become cleaner than they had been in decades. Yet in other regions, pollution worsened, and oil prices still continued to climb.

The world's **emerging economies**—especially China, India, and parts of Latin America—were growing fast. The people in these regions were buying more cars, and their industries needed more fuel. Many of these countries lacked strong environmental controls and for this reason they have some of the worst air quality in the world. Their need for oil, combined with that of the established economies of North America, Europe, and Japan, is now driving the most intense search for oil in the history of the world.

Earth's climate is experiencing one of the most dramatic changes in its history. This phenomenon, known as **global climate change** (or **global warming**), has seen Earth's average temperature increase by 1.4 degrees Fahrenheit (0.8 degrees Celsius) over the past hundred years. These temperatures are expected to rise another 2 to 11.5 degrees F (1.1 to 6.4 degrees C) during the next century. Many serious problems, such as melting glaciers and polar ice; rising sea levels; and severe heat waves, floods, and droughts have resulted from global climate change. Most environmental scientists believe that the primary cause of global climate change is human activity, especially the release of greenhouse gases such as **carbon dioxide**, into the atmosphere. Greenhouse gases have many sources, but most are created by the burning of oil and other hydrocarbon-based fuels to produce energy.

This search for more energy sources is introducing oil exploration and production to areas where it was previously unknown or thought to be unreachable. It is also driving the development of new techniques of oil extraction. Each of these historic developments has brought about benefits as well as problems, the most serious being the growing phenomenon of global climate change.

The air quality in many parts of the world is now so poor that people—like this family in Tokyo, Japan—must wear face masks when they go outside.

CRITICAL THINKING

- Imagine today's world without oil. How do you think your life would be different? Are there things that are important to you that would not exist?

- What other sources of energy and other natural resources could have been used in place of oil?

- How important was the oil industry's role in making the United States the leading world power it is today?

Many common house-hold items, like this tricycle, are made from oil-based products.

Chapter 2

The Benefits of Oil

Oil is so important in today's world that it is almost impossible to imagine life without it. But in recent years, economic factors and environmental concerns have led many to question the level of human reliance on oil as an energy source. Others, for many of the same reasons, continue to defend the use of this natural resource.

The most important use of oil is as an energy source. Almost 80 percent of the oil produced in the United States goes into fuels, specifically gasoline, which alone uses 47 percent of all U.S. oil production. Additional uses include aviation fuel, heating oil, and propane, which fuels backyard grills. Oil is required for the production of several other products, such as chemicals, plastics, asphalt for road construction, lubricants for machinery and medicines, and even as an additive in food for animals.

An Essential Element of Modern Life

The most important argument in favor of the continued use of oil is also the simplest: "We have no choice." So much of the world's economy and infrastructure relies on oil and oil-based products that any attempt to

A DEEPER DIVE

Economic Factors

There is no question that oil, and the oil industry, make important contributions to the U.S. and world economies. One major research study concluded that in 2010, the oil and natural gas industry contributed $476 billion to the U.S. economy. The industry makes this contribution through efforts that include employing large numbers of people; investing in infrastructure necessary for exploration; and making tax and other payments (such as lease payments for drilling on public lands) to federal, state, and local governments.

The greatest economic concern for many Americans is employment. Today the oil and natural gas industries provide jobs for about 10 million people, directly or indirectly. In fact, the U.S. areas that have extensive petroleum deposits also have some of the lowest unemployment rates. Oil companies in North Dakota's Bakken oil field, which has huge deposits of oil and especially natural gas, have found it difficult to locate qualified workers. Many positions in the industry pay very well. In fact, an oil worker in Alaska, for example, may earn $14,000 per month, more than four times the national average.

In some areas, many unemployed people are looking for scarce jobs (left). But in oil-rich regions like North Dakota (right), employers often have trouble finding enough workers.

The oil industry brings jobs, but also environmental risks, as shown by this oil rig, which ran aground off the Alaskan coast in 2012.

eliminate it from people's daily lives would be nothing short of impossible. Simply reducing the amounts of oil used by switching to alternative energy sources is extremely difficult and expensive, and could damage the economy. That is an extremely important issue, especially today.

The most recent economic recession, which began in 2008, proved to be the worst in more than half a century. It caused high unemployment in most parts of the world, including the United States. Although the U.S. economy seems to be recovering slowly, the job market is still tough. By the end of 2013, there were about six unemployed people for every job available. Under such difficult economic conditions, it is not easy to consider measures that could potentially make the job market worse.

An Abundance of Oil

Another important argument in favor of the use of oil is that far more of this resource is available than was previously known. Oil deposits have now been discovered in places where its presence was once only suspected, such as Brazil, Cuba, and the island of São Tomé off the west coast of Africa. Most industry experts no longer have concerns about peak oil, because it is now clear that the world's oil reserves are vastly greater than was suspected even twenty or thirty years ago. The result is that, even with demand increasing dramatically, especially in the emerging economics, the world is not in any immediate danger of running out of oil.

The U.S. Energy Information Administration (EIA) estimated the world's known oil reserves at 642.2 billion barrels in 1980. By 2013, the EIA estimate was 1.25 trillion barrels.

Ironically, environmental damage caused by greenhouse gases is actually opening up new sources of oil. As Earth's temperature rises, the ice in the Arctic is melting. This dramatic change makes it possible for oil exploration and transportation in what has always been one of the world's most remote and inaccessible regions.

Interestingly, one of the reasons for the heightened participation in oil exploration is something that is generally considered a serious problem: the rising price of oil. Many of the oil reserves that are being tapped, or may be tapped someday, are in remote regions where the conditions for exploration, discovery, extraction, and transportation are extremely difficult. Many of them are also in unstable or war-torn regions, making industry activity even riskier and more expensive than usual. When oil prices were comparatively low, recovery of oil in these regions was not considered economically feasible. With today's prices being comparatively high, oil companies are unearthing oil in some of the world's most remote regions.

The high price of oil is also driving the use of production techniques that in the past were not considered economically viable. One of these techniques is the extraction of oil from tar sands. This is a mining process in which vast amounts of oil-drenched sand are removed from the ground. The oil is then separated from the sand in huge factories, to produce a type of fuel known as **synthetic crude**. The most important tar sands known today are found in the Athabasca region of western Canada. This region, with a potential production capacity of 170 million barrels, is believed to hold the world's largest-known reserves of oil. Tar sands oil is extremely expensive to produce. The Athabasca deposits only became economically viable in the 1990s when oil prices began to rise after a period of being comparatively low. Because Canada, unlike many of the oil-producing nations of the Middle East, is a geographically close and historically friendly neighbor of the United States, its oil fields have the potential to deliver a steady, secure supply of oil for many years to come.

The proposed Keystone XL pipeline, an extension of the existing Keystone pipeline, is intended to transport Canadian oil from the Athabasca tar sands, as well as oil from the Bakken field in North Dakota, to refineries along Texas' Gulf Coast. Keystone XL is a massive project that will take many years to complete and cost billions of dollars. The U.S. government has not yet approved the pipeline's construction. If the project is completed, it will create jobs and deliver tax revenues and other tax-related benefits in six states.

Another oil extraction technique, hydraulic fracturing, or "fracking," has become more widely used in recent years, because it promises to deliver huge amounts of energy. Fracking is a process in which large amounts of water, sand, and chemicals are pumped into the earth under high pressure. This pressure then forcibly creates cracks in the Earth's surface. These cracks then fill with liquid hydrocarbons, especially natural gas, and **shale oil**, which can be distilled into a fuel called kerogen. Fracking, like tar sands mining, is extremely expensive. Yet the use of this technique is opening up oil and gas reserves in unexpected places, including locations that were not known to have important petroleum deposits. It is also providing the United States with reliable energy sources that may not require the use of long transportation routes. This is another method that has become economically viable only because of the high price of oil.

Fracking makes it possible to extract oil and natural gas even in residential areas.

In a remarkable reversal, the United States, which once relied heavily on foreign oil, now produces so much oil that it is expected to become the world's largest exporter of the resource by 2014. China, once one of the world's poorest and most under-developed countries, now has so much industry and demand for energy that it has become the largest oil importer.

Advances in drilling techniques are making it possible for oil companies to explore beneath the world's oceans. Approximately

As modern cities rise in emerging economies like China, the demand for oil increases dramatically.

70 percent of Earth's surface is covered with water, beneath which lies a great amount of the world's oil reserves. The first offshore oil wells were in very shallow water, and were built on wharves projecting from the land. Modern oil-drilling rigs, by comparison, can drill farther from shore, work in deeper waters, and control multiple oil wells. *The Perdido*, for example, can be operated almost 200 miles (322 kilometers) out in the Gulf of Mexico and in more than 9,500 feet (2,896 m) of water. Some offshore drills can now reach oil deposits almost two miles (3.2 km) beneath the ocean floor.

Oil Alternatives: Promise and Problems

Another important factor driving the world's continued reliance on oil and other petroleum products is the fact that many of the alternatives present serious problems. Many of these sources are currently under development, but not all are suitable as replacements for oil's most important use: fuel for automobiles, aircraft, and other vehicles. **Solar power** and **wind power**, for example, are beginning to be widely used in some parts of the world, especially in Europe, to generate electricity. Although these energy sources hold promise for heating and lighting many of the world's homes and businesses, they are not practical for use

A deep-sea drilling rig being prepared for operations in the Gulf of Mexico.

Wind turbines producing electricity in Oregon.

in vehicles. Another alternative is biofuel, a type of energy derived from renewable plant and animal materials. In the United States, federal law requires that all gasoline contain ethanol, a fuel additive made from corn. This is intended to reduce the amount of petroleum used by vehicles. Approximately 10 percent of U.S. gasoline content is now ethanol. (Some cars and trucks, known as flexible-fuel vehicles, can run on a range of fuels containing up to 85 percent ethanol.) Growing and transporting corn and ethanol requires the use of oil-powered farm and transportation vehicles. For this reason, the environmental impact of the use of biofuel may not be as positive as some people hope.

Efforts are under way to reduce the amount of oil used in automobiles, the greatest consumers of fuel. The available alternatives, however, continue to present significant problems. The simplest solution is the use of smaller, more fuel-efficient vehicles. But many people, especially in the United States, prefer automobiles with more powerful, more fuel-consuming engines. Other alternatives, from **diesel** engines to hybrid cars to all-electric vehicles, remain significantly more expensive than conventional automobiles. Some have other limitations. All-electric vehicles, for example, can travel about 100 miles (161 km) before needing to be recharged, which makes them impractical for people who need to drive long distances. They also require a nationwide network of charging stations, but to date, few have been built.

Another problem with employing alternatives is the growing recognition that even though carbon emissions from oil are extremely

About 40 percent of the corn raised in the United States is now used for fuel.

damaging to the environment, some other energy sources are even worse. The coal industry, for example, supplies 37 percent of U.S. electricity, more than any other source. The areas where it is mined, such as the Appalachian Mountains of Kentucky and West Virginia, have long suffered environmental devastation. Coal mining sometimes leaves huge open pits in the ground. Mining companies even remove entire mountaintops in their search for coal. Industrial waste from mining operations is often dumped in rivers and lakes, polluting water supplies. Most importantly, when coal is burned, it produces some of the world's worst air pollution. This is one of the reasons that emerging economies, such as China and India, which use older and less-efficient coal-dependent power plants, have such poor air quality.

It is not only environmentalists who are worried about another source of energy that the world has relied heavily on for more than sixty years:

The radiation risk from the damaged nuclear power plant in Fukushima, Japan is so great that anyone who goes there must wear protective clothing.

nuclear energy. Nuclear power plants represent a highly efficient means of producing electricity, yet there is deep concern about the plants' potential for environmental disaster. These fears deepened significantly in 2011 when an earthquake and tsunami severely damaged nuclear reactors in Fukushima, Japan. Following the disaster, **radiation** leaked into the air, soil, and water in the region. Dangerously high levels were discovered in food grown and fish caught in the area. The Japanese government, concluding that nuclear power was simply too dangerous, announced plans to close all its nuclear power plants. (Several European countries are also reconsidering their uses of nuclear power. Germany, for example, plans to close all of its nuclear power plants by 2022.) This decision has sharply reduced electrical output in Japan, a country that has almost no natural energy resources of its own, and severely damaged the country's economy. Even today, Japan is desperately trying to find other energy sources, and is buying oil and other fuels from suppliers all over the world. This competition for supply is just one more factor in the high price of oil worldwide.

Because it is so central to people's lives, oil is a resource that cannot simply be abandoned. We can, however, work to reduce our dependence on it, specifically on oil from unreliable foreign sources. But we will definitely need it, and need it in large amounts, for many years to come.

CRITICAL THINKING

- Will the discovery of new sources of oil encourage people and businesses to use even more of this resource?

- Is the high cost of oil a good thing, a bad thing, or both?

- Should the United States focus on locating sources of oil closer to home, or continue to explore more distant regions, or both?

Crude oil spilled from a ruptured tank in South Korea.

Chapter 3

The True Cost of Oil

For many years, one of the primary concerns about the world's heavy reliance on oil has been the fear that it would simply run out. This concern about peak oil now seems exaggerated, because newly discovered deposits and newly developed extraction techniques have dramatically increased its potential supply. But this does not mean that the supply problem no longer exists. In fact, it remains a very serious one for the entire world. One important reason is that many of the new sources of oil are found in remote and distant parts of the world, that is, remote deserts, impenetrable jungles, and deep waters. This makes finding, extracting, and transporting oil extremely expensive.

A deep-sea drilling rig, for example, may cost an oil company as much as $3 billion to build, put in place, and operate before it delivers a single barrel of oil. Some oil wells, on land and at sea, never produce any oil, so most of the money invested in those unproductive wells is wasted. Some economists believe that extracting oil from the high Arctic may cost as much as $100 per barrel. At current prices, this would not be profitable. And the farther the well is from the refinery where its oil will be processed, the more expensive it is to transport. Those additional costs

A nuclear-powered Russian icebreaker makes its way through the high Arctic.

are passed on to the consumer in the price of everyday commodities from a plastic bottle of shampoo to a gallon of gasoline.

The Rising Cost of Oil

In 1999, many drivers in the United States were shocked when, for the first time, the average price of gasoline exceeded $1.00 per gallon (about $0.25 per L). But by 2008, prices had climbed to more than $4.00 per gallon (about $1.00 per L) in many parts of the country.

Every dollar that is spent on oil or oil-based products is a dollar that cannot be spent on anything else. When the price of gasoline increases, families have less money to spend on everything from housing to food to children's toys. This makes life more difficult for consumers who need to purchase such products and services. It also harms the businesses that provide these products, as well as their employees, who may lose their jobs when business is bad.

The high price of oil hurts businesses in other ways, too. When a company pays more for fuel and other oil-based products, it has less money to invest in developing new products and hiring new employees. Rising oil prices have hurt many businesses in recent years. Airlines and trucking and shipping companies, for example, have been forced to raise their prices to pay for skyrocketing fuel costs. This has resulted in increased prices for everything from oranges grown in Florida to televisions manufactured in Korea. This leads to a phenomenon that some economists call an "oil ceiling," in which the high cost of oil keeps the world economy from recovering from its long downturn.

The high price of oil is not the only cause of unfavorable economic impacts. Price volatility—the high-to-low swing of oil prices in recent years—makes it extremely difficult for consumers, businesses, and even governments to plan ahead. People are unsure as to whether they can afford to purchase a new home or car, manufacturers cannot decide whether to build new factories, and governments cannot predict the amount of tax revenue they will have to spend.

Much of this volatility is caused by the uncertainty of oil supplies, which is often the result of political problems outside the United States. In the past four decades, for example, five major wars have been fought in the Middle East, the region that has historically been the world's most important source of oil. Most of those wars have resulted in either shortages or deep concerns about shortages. The result has been periods of high oil prices that last weeks, months, or even years.

Price volatility also results in problems much closer to home. There is no question that the oil industry creates jobs, many of which are highly paid. The "ripple effect" from the industry spreads far beyond those employed within the industry. The wages from their jobs pay for houses and cars, and taxes paid by both employer and employee help to fund schools, highways, and public services. But the industry's economic impact is not so simple. Many of those jobs, whether in the oil fields on the North Slope of Alaska or the refineries on the Gulf of Mexico, are extremely uncertain. From its earliest days, the oil industry has been a "boom-or-bust" business, quickly moving from bustling activity and high employment to low prices and devastated local economies.

Many oil-producing regions are concerned about potential depletion of their reserves and the resulting economic impact. Some experts believe, for example, that the remaining oil reserves in Saudi Arabia, which derives more than 90 percent of its economic output from the oil industry, are much lower than previously thought. The country has few other natural resources and minimal industry, and will need to find other ways to drive its economy.

The reality is that oil wealth is rarely evenly distributed. Many countries in the Middle East, for example, have become rich from oil extraction, but the wealth has remained in relatively few hands. In Saudi Arabia, even as the price of oil has skyrocketed, the standard of living for the average citizen has fallen sharply. One reason is that the engineers and the other highly skilled professionals who design and build oil drilling operations are often foreigners. This bitter disparity between the oil-rich few and the rest of the population also gives rise to conflicts. Oil exploration has historically been a precursor of political unrest.

Oil wealth has fueled great economic growth in many countries, but this wealth does not usually reach ordinary people, such as the migrant workers shown here in Dubai.

The bitterness of exploited peoples, who witness the riches from their natural resources effectively being stolen, leads to conflict, war, and even terrorism.

The huge oil industry in the West African nation of Nigeria, for example, has created great wealth for a few of its citizens, but most Nigerians are still very poor. Many are so desperate for heating or cooking fuel that they illegally "tap into" the pipelines that crisscross the areas where they live. This is an extremely dangerous practice and has caused fires and explosions that have resulted in the deaths of thousands.

A DEEPER DIVE

Dangerous Work

The oil industry has always been dirty, dangerous work, both for the people performing the tasks and for those living in the surrounding areas. Since the earliest days of the Pennsylvania oil fields, thousands of oil workers have been killed in fires, explosions, and other mining-related accidents. The worst loss of life during an oil disaster came in 1988 when the *Piper Alpha*, a drilling rig in the North Sea off Scotland, caught fire and exploded, killing 122 people. Transporting oil, whether by pipeline, truck, or rail, has always been dangerous, too. In July 2013, a freight train carrying oil derailed and exploded in the small Canadian town of Lac-Mégantic. The town's center was almost completely destroyed, and forty-seven people were killed instantly. Disasters like these have always been sadly common, and seem likely to continue.

Oil and the Government

Another economic factor that must be taken into account when considering arguments against oil is government subsidies. Even though the oil industry is hugely profitable—ExxonMobil, for example, is the world's largest company—governments worldwide provide oil companies tax breaks and outright payments to support their efforts in finding and extracting oil. Citizens' tax dollars support these oil-company benefits and must be considered as one of the costs of our reliance on oil. The economic impacts of the oil industry are not as simple, and not as entirely positive, as one might think. But economic problems are not the strongest arguments against the continued dependence on oil.

The world's dependence on oil has also contributed to political conflict and violence in several regions throughout the world. Many people in the Middle East, for example, believe that the United States and other western powers have interfered in their internal politics to protect their oil supplies as well as profits that come from oil. Their resentment has led, directly or indirectly, to violent protests and even terrorist attacks and wars. Moreover, many countries, such as Venezuela, are now determined to take greater control of their oil production. This may mean that they choose to sell their oil in other markets, so that less of their production flows to the United States.

Oil exploration has the potential to increase conflict in unexpected areas. The high Arctic, for example, is claimed by several different countries, including the United States, Russia, and Canada. As the Arctic ice melts due to climate change, oil exploration in the region becomes more feasible. As a result, the potential for conflict, and possibly even war, over valuable natural resources increases.

United States Air Force fighter jets fly over Kuwaiti oil fields set on fire by retreating Iraqi forces in 1991.

The Effect of Oil on the Environment

The most compelling argument against our continued dependence on the oil industry relates to the harsh damage it causes to the environment. Oil is poisonous in even very small amounts. It can contaminate the air we breathe, the water we drink, and the food we eat. It is potentially dangerous to the environment at every stage: exploration, discovery, extraction, transportation, and use.

Many forms of oil production and transportation can pollute both air and water. Oil disasters, especially those that take place at sea, can dump millions of gallons of crude oil into sensitive ecosystems such as the Gulf of Mexico. Oil pipelines sometimes leak, resulting in the possible contamination of the underground sources of water for millions of people. Past oil tanker accidents have severely damaged coastlines in many parts of the world.

Many types of oil production yield enormous amounts of harmful air pollution. A recent study in Canada found that carcinogens, substances that can cause cancers, are now 300 times more prevalent in the air downwind from the Athabasca tar sands than in other areas. This increase in pollution may result in higher incidences of serious diseases in the future.

Some of the newest forms of oil extraction are especially dangerous to the environment. The process of extracting oil from the tar sands requires enormous amounts of oil to fuel the factories performing the extracting. Even more importantly, the process destroys millions of acres of land, one area being the boreal forest in the Athabasca region. It also produces extraordinary amounts of carbon dioxide and other pollutants that foul the air. This all contributes to the filth in the environment and, crucially, to global climate change.

A DEEPER DIVE

The Economic Impact of Environmental Damage

The oil industry's environmental impact has important economic consequences. These may include the increased health costs of treating people who become ill because of environmental pollution and the staggering expenses of recovering from an environmental disaster. The *Deepwater Horizon* oil spill, for example, fouled the beaches along the Gulf of Mexico, severely damaging the important tourist industry. It also made fishing in many parts of the Gulf unsafe. These economic impacts on outside parties, which economists call externalities, are extremely difficult to calculate. It has, however, been reported that BP, one of the companies involved in the disaster, has set aside $100 billion for recovery efforts, lawsuits, fines, and other costs for Gulf restoration. The total cost of the physical damages is certainly far higher than $100 billion, however.

The Athabasca oil sands in western Canada.

Using Less Oil

It is important to remember that many ways of reducing dependence on oil exist. While some are difficult, expensive, and even inconvenient, they can actually cut costs for people and businesses. Many homeowners, especially those in sunny environments such as the American Southwest, have installed rooftop solar panels. These panels produce electricity that reduces or even eliminates heating and air-conditioning costs, including those from burning oil. Increasing the insulation in a building can dramatically reduce the amount of energy consumed. Simply painting the roof of a house white reflects the sun's rays and cools the house. This reduces the amount of fuel necessary to maintain comfortable indoor temperatures during the summer months. The most important efforts in reducing or eliminating oil dependence lie in altering its most common use: transportation.

In several parts of the world, especially in some European countries, many drivers are switching to cars powered by diesel engines. Diesel, which has long been the preferred fuel for trucks and other heavy vehicles, is significantly more fuel-efficient than gasoline. Diesel-powered cars and diesel fuel are both more expensive than their conventional equivalents, yet their drivers can save as much as 30 percent on overall fuel costs. This is making the cars more attractive to buyers in the United States, even though the increased demand has raised the price of diesel fuel in recent years.

Many other projects are under way to develop and market vehicles that run on alternative fuels. These include cars that use hydrogen, either as a combustible fuel or to power electric fuel cells, as well as cars that run on

Energy-efficient hybrid cars, like this one, are an increasingly common sight on the world's highways.

natural gas and other types of fuel. Some drivers have converted their cars to run on vegetable oils, such as those used for cooking. In some areas drivers are even stealing waste oils from restaurant garbage containers to fuel their cars. Researchers in South Korea report that they have actually been able to produce small amounts of commercial-grade gasoline from E. coli, an extremely dangerous form of bacteria that causes serious, sometimes fatal, food poisoning.

The most successful fuel-saving vehicle on America's roads today is likely the hybrid model, which has two engines: one that is electric and another that is gasoline-powered. A hybrid engine runs on electricity at lower speeds, usually up to about 40 miles (64 kilometers) per hour. As the speed increases, it switches to the gasoline engine, which powers the car, but also recharges its battery. Hybrids have become more popular

Many people, like these cyclists in the city of Amsterdam in the Netherlands, prefer to get around without using oil at all.

despite being more expensive to buy than conventional cars.

Even though the purchase price of gasoline in the United States has in recent years been at historical highs, Americans still pay far less at the pump than people in many other countries. In oil-rich Norway, for example, drivers were paying the equivalent of almost $10.00 per gallon ($2.50 per liter) in 2013, compared with an average of just under $4.00 in the United States. The main reason for this disparity in pricing is high government taxes designed to strongly encourage Norwegians to drive more fuel-efficient vehicles.

Some manufacturers have moved beyond the hybrid concept, designing and building fuel-less all-electric cars. This model does have disadvantages: high cost, limited range, and a limited number of charging stations. Yet they are steadily becoming more popular. The Tesla, for example, despite its high sticker price, is now the best-selling car in Norway. The more affordable Nissan Leaf, a small all-electric car, is beginning to appear on America's highways more often. The potential role that electric vehicles will play in the automotive market is unclear, but they are probably here to stay. And, crucially, both hybrid and all-electric vehicles are considered zero-emission, which means that their use does not contribute significantly to air pollution.

There are ways of reducing oil dependence that do not involve purchasing replacement vehicles. One way, for example, is to transport more people via trains and buses. A train uses far more energy than a car, but unlike a car, it can move hundreds, even thousands, of people. Investment in mass transit would aid in the reduction of both energy consumption and pollution. One of the simplest forms of mechanical transportation, the bicycle, is likely also the most environmentally friendly of all. It requires no fuel and does not contribute to pollution in any way. Many cities worldwide have created special routes to help cyclists ride to work or just get fresh air and exercise.

It is also important to remember that finding alternatives to oil is not only a source of cost, but also a source of economic opportunity. The development of alternative energy sources and the uses for them will require a great deal of work. The skills necessary to perform this level of work have not yet been defined or developed. Some of these economic opportunities are more promising than those that are traditional. Following the recession that began in 2008, conventional car sales decreased in most parts of the world. This was due in part to the high cost of fuel. One segment of the automotive industry that remained strong was the manufacturers of hybrid cars. Factories that manufacture hybrids—along with solar panels, wind turbines, and many other so-called **green technologies**—offered high salaries to skilled workers.

Perhaps the strongest argument against relying so heavily on oil is that it will keep us from making serious efforts to find alternatives. Alternative energy sources and technologies are available, and many others are on the horizon. Finding and developing them, and making their use widespread will be difficult, time consuming, and expensive, however. The efforts to replace oil, or at least to reduce the amounts used, will require tremendous collective efforts on the part of governments, businesses, and ordinary people. As long as oil is readily available, or at least seems to be, there is less incentive to make that effort.

CRITICAL THINKING

- What can oil-producing areas do to prepare for the day when their oil resources are depleted, or oil prices fall?
- Do you think your family has been affected by the high price of oil in recent years? If so, how?
- Should governments enforce regulations and taxes to encourage oil exploration, or encourage reductions in the use of oil, or both?

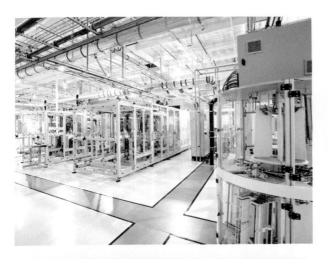

Solar panels being manufactured, inspected, and installed.

Oil is here to stay.

The Future of Oil

Chapter 4

It is clear that the world will not be able to give up using oil for many years to come, if ever. It may not be possible to reduce reliance on this fuel source, or even slow the growth in demand. Many industry observers, from the International Energy Agency to OPEC, believe that demand will continue to increase for many years. The oil company BP has estimated that oil demand, which currently stands at 89 billion barrels per day, will increase to 104 billion per day by 2030.

Not everyone agrees with this forecast, however. There are actually signs that worldwide demand may be slowing. The developing countries, especially China and India, need more and more oil as their industries expand and their citizens are able to afford automobiles. But in the developed world, demand for oil has decreased since 2005. While there are many reasons for this, the high price of fuel is certainly one of the most important. This has caused drivers to demand, and manufacturers to supply, more efficient vehicles. Many are constructed from lighter materials and have engines that require less hydrocarbon-based fuel, or none at all.

A 2013 model vehicle sold in the United States averaged 24.9 miles per gallon (10.6 km per L). Although this represents greatly overall improved mileage, the Environmental Protection Agency (EPA) has set a target average of 35.5 miles per gallon (15 km per L) for all new vehicles in 2016, and 54.5 miles per gallon (23 km per L) for 2025. The enforcement of these targets will help to reduce demand for oil in the United States. It will also benefit the environment, by reducing the amount of carbon dioxide in the atmosphere.

The Value of Fuel-Efficient Vehicles

There are many reasons to support the trend toward more fuel-efficient vehicles. The price of fuel, for example, has caused many people to rethink purchasing gas-guzzling automobiles. These decisions have also been driven by government action, specifically regulations demanding that manufacturers create more fuel-efficient vehicles and lower greenhouse gas emissions. In many parts of the world, high taxes on gasoline and other fuels are helping to cut oil consumption.

Another reason some observers believe that the demand for oil will slow is the explosive growth in natural gas production from both fracking and conventional techniques. Converting machinery to natural gas is less expensive than some of the other alternatives. It is unclear whether the use of natural gas would reduce greenhouse gas emissions, or by how much. However, because large amounts of natural gas are being found and recovered in the United States, it can potentially reduce our reliance on foreign oil.

Worldwide government action is clearly needed to reduce both demand for oil and its environmental impacts. The U.S. government is not the only body working to reduce oil consumption. In fact, it lags well behind some others. In the European Union (EU), a group of twenty-two mostly wealthy countries, regulations and taxes have raised average vehicle mileage ratings to almost double that of the United States. One important result of this action is that 30 percent of cars sold in the EU are considered low-emission vehicles, which produce comparatively small amounts of greenhouse gases.

Governments worldwide clearly recognize the importance of both reducing their dependence on expensive, unreliable sources of oil and limiting the release of environmentally disastrous greenhouse gases from hydrocarbons into the atmosphere. Many proposals have been made to encourage governments to take stronger actions.

Government Action and Personal Choice

The United Nations (UN) has held a series of climate change conferences in Japan, Qatar, and South Africa to set targets for the amounts of carbon dioxide different countries will emit and agree on ways to meet those targets. (The next conference is scheduled to be held in France in 2015.) The negotiations during these conferences have been very difficult, and have not yet resulted in much concrete action. They have, however, increased public awareness of global climate change and the urgent need to take action to reverse it, if possible.

Many proposals have been presented as ways to reduce both hydrocarbon consumption and greenhouse gas emissions. One is known as "cap and trade." In this system, a polluter—a factory or car manufacturer for example—receives a permit from the government to produce a certain amount (the "cap") of greenhouse gas. If the polluter produces more than

Solving global climate change will require cooperation from people all over the world.

EXECUTIVE SECRETARY

PRESIDENT

the allowed amount, it needs to "trade" with another permit holder, paying it for the right to pollute more. This gives both parties in the system a strong financial incentive to reduce the amounts of greenhouse gas they produce. The EU has a strong cap-and-trade system in place, but this idea has not yet caught on in the United States, partly because it is so complex and difficult to enforce.

Another approach is known as a carbon tax. This is a government tax based on the amount of carbon dioxide emitted into the air by a particular type of carbon-based fuel. Carbon taxes are similar to the taxes most countries place on gasoline, but are more complicated because they vary depending on the fuel type. Diesel fuel, for example, is usually taxed at a lower rate, because modern diesel engines emit less carbon. Additionally, carbon taxes apply not only to cars and trucks, but also to factories and power plants. This is one reason that some countries that rely heavily on coal- and oil-powered electrical production—such as the United States, Russia, and China—are opposed to this approach.

All of these efforts, which are taking place at the international, national, local, and even personal levels, have the same basic goal: reducing carbon footprints. This term describes the amount of greenhouse gases—specifically carbon dioxide—that a person, a business, or even a country is responsible for sending into the atmosphere. The footprint is not limited to the amount of greenhouse gases produced by burning fuel in cars, furnaces, and other equipment that uses oil. It also measures the carbon used in the production of consumer items purchased and used. For example, recycling plastic shopping bags, or replacing them with paper, reduces the amount of carbon that is used.

Some methods of reducing carbon footprints rely heavily on technology. For example, drivers often waste time and fuel searching for

A motorist prepares to buy fuel at a gas station in Peoria, Illinois.

places to park in crowded public areas. New projects under way in cities from San Francisco to Beijing are exploring ways to resolve this problem through the use of mobile phone apps and sensors on parking meters that will alert drivers to available spaces. Some industry observers believe such projects could save one million barrels of oil per day worldwide.

Reducing greenhouse emissions is not just a matter of reducing oil consumption. In many parts of the world, serious efforts are under way to trap carbon and store it away from the atmosphere. This process, known as carbon sequestration, may involve removing carbon dioxide from the stacks of power plants. It may also involve removing carbon from the atmosphere and storing it in underground reservoirs. In one such project, in Port Arthur, Texas, carbon waste from a refinery is being turned into gases that can be reused in fracking operations. This can potentially make oil production more efficient and less expensive, and at the same time cut down on greenhouse gas emissions.

Despite the difficulties involved in getting large numbers of countries with opposing economic and political interests to agree on ways to reduce greenhouse gas emissions, important steps are already being taken. China, which is estimated to produce almost 25 percent of the world's carbon dioxide emissions, has announced that it may place limits on its carbon emissions beginning in 2016. While the Chinese government has not yet announced what those limits will be, it is an encouraging sign from a country that will soon be the world's largest economy. One key factor in this shift is China's increasing reliance on hydroelectricity and movement away from the use of coal power plants.

These developments are not only taking place in China but in many other parts of the world. A European report recently indicated that in

Simply walking to school, instead of driving, can be a step toward reducing our dependence on oil.

2012, carbon dioxide emissions increased at a rate less than half of the prior ten-year average. The report also showed that carbon dioxide emissions reached a record high of 38 billion tons in 2012, but that the worldwide increase was significantly lower than the rate of economic growth. The rate of emissions growth also shows promise, at least in some parts of the world. It was reported lower in the world's three largest economies: China, the United States, and the EU.

The encouraging fact about oil-saving efforts is that they are happening everywhere, and at all levels of citizenry. International organizations such as the UN are working to reach agreements on fuel production and consumption. Governments are also working independently to achieve the same goals.

Businesses, driven mostly by financial decisions, are exploring ways to reduce their fuel consumption. People are doing the same by employing methods as simple as driving smaller, more fuel-efficient cars, using public transportation, or walking to work or school.

What does all this mean for the future of oil? Certainly not that oil supplies will disappear. But it does mean that people should—and will—practice using this valuable resource more responsibly.

CRITICAL THINKING

- Do you think your generation will use more oil than previous generations, or less?
- Can you think of ways that you and your family can reduce your carbon footprint?
- What technologies will influence the ways we use oil in the future?

Glossary

by-product: something left over in the making of a product

calorie: a unit of measurement of energy equal to the approximate amount of heat required to raise the temperature of one gram of water one degree Celsius (1.8 degrees Fahrenheit)

carbon dioxide: a harmful chemical compound that is both created naturally and produced by the burning of hydrocarbons

cartel: a group of owners of a resource who work to limit competition and maintain high prices

diesel: a type of fuel, used in special engines, that is more energy-efficient than gasoline

distill: to purify a liquid by heating it until it becomes a gas and then cooling it until it returns to liquid form

ecosystem: the complex interaction of living things and their natural environment

emerging economy (developing economy): a country or region, previously poor and mostly agricultural, that is developing modern industry

energy content: the amount of energy produced by a specific amount of fuel; commonly expressed in a unit called a calorie

global climate change (or global warming): the process, largely caused by human activity, by which Earth's temperature is rapidly rising

green technology: technology designed to be less harmful to the environment than traditional methods

mineral: a solid, nonorganic substance that occurs naturally

natural gas: a mixture of hydrocarbon gases, often found close to oil deposits, and used as an energy source

nuclear energy: energy produced by radiation

peak oil: the theoretical point when the world's demand for oil exceeds the supply

radiation: a form of energy (sometimes, but not always, harmful) that can travel through space and some materials

refinery: a place where oil or other hydrocarbons are processed into useable products

renewable resource: a resource (for example, solar power) that continues to occur naturally

shale oil: oil extracted from rock formation by processes such as hydraulic fracturing

solar power: energy gathered from sunlight by solar panels

synthetic: made by humans and not occurring in nature

synthetic crude: a form of crude oil mined from tar sands

wind power: energy gathered from the wind; for example by turbines

Find Out More

Books

Challoner, Jack. *Energy*. London, England: Dorling Kindersley, 2012.

Gardner, Timothy. *Oil*. Diminishing Resources. Greensboro, NC: Morgan Reynolds Publishing, 2010.

Landau, Elaine. *The History of Energy*. Minneapolis, MN: Twenty-First Century Books, 2006.

Mercer, Ian. *Oils and the Environment.* Mankato, MN: Stargazer Books, 2005.

Ollhoff, Jim. *Fossil Fuels, Future Energy*. Edina, MN: ABDO Publishing Company, 2010.

Websites

Climate Change: Basic Information —
United States Environmental Protection Agency
www.epa.gov/climatechange/basics

This website, from the U.S. government agency responsible for the environment, discusses the problem of global climate change and possible solutions. The "Students' Site" section includes games and other activities, including a carbon emission calculator.

Energy Kids (Oil) —
United States Energy Information Administration
www.eia.gov/kids/energy.cfm?page=oil_home-basics

This U.S. government site offers detailed information on the history of the oil industry, and includes resources and activities for both students and teachers.

Energy Star Kids
www.energystar.gov/index.cfm?c=kids.kids_index

This interactive site has information, games, and other activities focusing on ways to reduce energy consumption and protect the environment.

Extreme Oil — PBS
www.pbs.org/wnet/extremeoil/index.html

A companion to a public television series broadcast in 2004 (and available on DVD), *Extreme Oil* explores the history of oil from prehistoric times to the present.

Index

Page numbers in **boldface** are illustrations.

About the Author

Terry Allan Hicks is a longtime business and technology writer who has published more than twenty nonfiction books for young readers, on subjects ranging from Native American history to the solar system. He lives in Connecticut with his wife, Nancy, and their sons, James, John, and Andrew.